Kneeling Orion

KNEELING ORION

POEMS BY
Kate Barnes

WOODCUTS BY
Mary Azarian

DAVID R. GODINE
PUBLISHER · BOSTON

First published in 2004 by
David R. Godine, Publisher
Post Office Box 450
Jaffrey, New Hampshire 03452
www.godine.com

The poems in *Kneeling Orion* originally appeared in the following publications:
The Alaska Quarterly, *The American Scholar*, *The Beloit Poetry Journal*,
The Café Review, *The Cream City Review*, *The Green Mountains Review*,
The Harvard Review, *The Kenyon Review*, *The New England Review*,
The New Yorker, *Orion*, *Persephone*, *Rivendell*,
Sipapu, and *Yankee Magazine*.

LIBRARY OF CONGRESS
CATALOGING-IN-PUBLICATION DATA
Barnes, Kate, 1932–
Kneeling Orion / by Kate Barnes; woodcuts by Mary Azarian
p. cm.
ISBN 1–56792–255–4 (alk. paper)
1. New England—Poetry. I. Title.
PS355.A6812K58 2003
811´.54—dc21 2003013722

FIRST EDITION
Printed in Canada

This book is
for Eleanor Mattern,
the one reader any poem
would wish to have.

CONTENTS

Knowing the Goddess Epona

Why Do You Ask?

"The Rhetoric of Fiction"

Kneeling Orion

The Story She Knew

The Story She Knew

for Rob Farnsworth

Clouds above the calm sea
trail their reflections all the way in
from the islands, just as sloops
stand over their own sails
so lengthened on water that they look
like ribbons of light, endless.

One early morning
in May (it was long ago)
a girl with black hair galloped alone
on a small bay horse through the deer park
near Copenhagen. The young beech leaves
reached out their earliest green, the oak trees
stood waiting, a thousand years old. Herds
of white fallow deer rose from their beds
among the ferns, and streamed away
like water foaming over a stone dam
in spring rain.

This was a story
I thought I knew already. I felt certain
the deer came from the margins of a book
called *History* that told many sorrows, the falls
of empires, great kingdoms
sown with salt – although the letters
seemed to dance on the pages
as I read them. The new leaves
hung from the trees, half-folded, and I was sure
I could feel the world still holding its breath
all around me when my lover's body
sank into mine, the same breath
it holds when a swan rears his heavy breast
high over the water, getting ready

to kick his way into the air, while a being
made out of nothing but radiance
stretches far beneath him
on the black surface; the same pause
it makes for a long, long moment
before the last contraction that brings the child –
compressed, bloody, not yet breathing –
into the flooding light.

The Kitchen Window

The eleven-year-old girl whose light brown hair
looped in strong curls sat easily
bareback on a large black and white pony
with staring blue eyes, a pony like a prophet
in the form of a small horse. She rode around
the island of brush in the driveway – toyons,
wild lilacs – and disappeared.
                                        What was I wishing
for her while I stood at the kitchen window,
my hands in the full sink, my thoughts
following her as she dropped away
into the shadows of the oak grove? I can't remember
exactly. Common dreams, no doubt, easy graces
that would make her queen some day of a small kingdom
where grief could never get in.
                              Hah!
                                        I was still
a child myself then, a dreaming child, clinging
to the moving shadows of leaves
on a warm wall. I was planting
roses, I was singing lullabies
about a bleating lamb, I was telling endless
fairy tales – as if anyone ever
lived happily ever after, as if the fearful twist
of sadness and betrayal didn't twine
through everything, even the brightest threads
of light...
              But never mind
all that, never mind the way
we learn, and the day darkens, and things
come out differently. I've returned
to the kitchen window now, I'm watching

the pony's tail, black and white like a magpie's wing,
swinging behind as he sinks from sight
under the outstretched branches.
                              And so the ghost
goes back to washing her dishes, the ghost
of a young woman who has no trouble creating
a world of glittering, pure, unbroken
happiness when she thinks how the April morning,
so full of running streams and green, new leaves,
was made to be ridden through, and her child
is riding through it for her.

Old Roses

When my father met my mother
at a dinner party in a garden of very old roses
on Beacon Hill one hot evening
in early June, he said to his friend, F. Morton
Smith, that night, "Morton, I have met
the girl I'm going to marry!"
                              (We have Uncle Morton's
testimony for that, the certified word
of a Boston lawyer.)
                        My mother
said my father had looked handsome, yes,
and talked delightfully, but what *she* remembered
were the mosquitoes. "If you stopped slapping at them,
even for a second, you were eaten up
alive."
        My father courted her
for the next ten years, whenever they found themselves
in the same place. It was the twenties then,
heyday of ocean liners, and she might be
in Paris, or maybe off getting
run away with by a hairy, two-humped camel
in the Gobi Desert, while he was crossing
the Pyrenees on foot; but, at last, on another
steamy hot day in Massachusetts, as she,
still wet from the bath, lay naked upstairs
on her sister's bed, she heard the wedding march
start up on the grand piano
directly below her. She sprang to her feet,
threw on her cream-colored dress with a dipping hemline,
and flung herself down the narrow old staircase
straight into the arms of matrimony – which were wearing

an English jacket of dark blue wool for the occasion,
splendid, but unendurable.
                                        Would anyone say
the marriage was a happy one? I don't think
I know. Sometimes. Perhaps. I can't imagine
either of them with anyone else. Years later, I,
a greedy child, crouched in the dark cabinet
under the attic stairs, and wolfed down
the last slice of their wedding-cake, dried out fruitcake
in a little box covered with silver paper
and lined with paper lace, a keepsake
for wedding guests to slip under their pillows
that night so that they, too, would dream the bright moon
rolling her way through silver light, singing stars
clustering under the clouds.
                                        Those crumbs
became the bones in my seven-year-old body –
and they're in there yet – while the dreams
sing on in my head forever, like mosquitoes
whining among the leaves of thorny old roses.

Henry (Sheahan) Beston

Shamed for being a mick, my young father changed his name
from one meaning "fairy hill" to one that meant "by the stone."

Fair woman, will you go with me to a wonderful land where music is?
Every hill there is purple, the blackbirds' eggs delight the eye.

In the dark barn the horse named "Who?" seems to glow like a huge
    ruby,
lit from within. On his brow there is a small question mark.

Holinshed, in 1560, said the Irish were querulous and frank,
great sorcerers, great horsemen, open-handed, "passing in hospitalitie."

"Words are all we have," wrote Beckett, who also called every word
"an unnecessary strain on silence and nothingness."

"I will leave," sings my father in the hall, "I will go away,
and I will never come back except as foam on the shore."

American Women

I

"American women!"
said my father
often and bitterly.

All his unhappiness
was in the phrase,
the great anger

that life was unfair —
to him, to him —
I can hear it yet.

The message in it
was for my mother:
"Castrating bitches."

Of course, he would never
have used those words.
He didn't have to;

she knew what he meant.
She said nothing.
She looked sad and bore it,

but went on offending
by writing more books.

II

I, too,
a ten-year-old future
American woman,

heard it all
and in that agreeable
house of books

and gardens, the lawn
yielding to hayfields,
the fields

to the lake, the lake
to reflected clouds —
breathed in

the whole thing, his rage
and grief, her grief
and silent answer.

III

Sitting on the old
merry-go-round
horse in the shed-

loft, I wondered:
wasn't it my fault?
Right after

I was born,
my father had come
to my mother's bedside

in a storm of tears —
once again, no son.

IV

At ten, I hadn't
heard that story,
but perhaps I felt it

anyway. I spent
a lot of my time
in attics. When people

called me, I wouldn't breathe
or answer. I wished
I could be invisible,

an invisible child,
or perhaps only

an unconceived,
wandering, unrealized
spirit, a speck,

a spark, a shadow,
a twist of wind

in the standing hay.

The Farm

When I say "the farm" I mean
Chimney Farm, some land in Maine
      not far from here
where my parents, those quick spirits,
filled the place that now inherits
      all they were

through the shapely words they left,
each one tried for grip and heft,
      like a stone
lifted from among the tangle,
looked at well from every angle,
      then fitted in

to the miles of lines they raised
like stone walls, those lines that praised
      the loves they shared
for their red farmhouse and the green
fields around it, with the sheen
      that appeared

when the wind blew through the oaks
on the stone pile, and the spokes
      in the wide wheels
of the carts were no more blue
than the long lake that lay below
      where the keels

of canoe and rowboat slipped
through clear water as they dipped
          oar or light paddle
any summer afternoon,
calling to the watching loon
          whose wild yodel

they so often heard at night
as, by moonlight or stars' light,
          those bird souls flew
toward Deep Cove, above their heads,
while they lay warm in their beds
          and the slow

constellations wheeled the sky,
and their responsive lives went by,
          leaving their words
in a drift, a leap, a glitter,
a shape of stars that call and twitter
          like the small birds

we see flocking everywhere
now that September's in the air,
          getting ready
to travel their instinctive roads
through the shifting, wind-blown clouds,
          holding steady.

On the Highway Bridge

When I drive my car across the salt river
on the highway bridge, I look upstream
toward a wide bay opening out
among hayfields. Today the water
was a strong bluish-green, almost the color
of a beetle's back, although the sky
seemed light blue wherever I could see it
in the clefts of clouds; and the clouds
rose up as feathered towers, castles
of washed wool. Is that Heaven? No,
it's only one more demonstration
of mutability.
          Asleep,
I drove two white mares by a darker river
in a strange city. Were you there? I can't
tell now because of the way my dreams
sail through the pale sky, changing.

The Porch

The willow through whose leaves the full moon
rose all summer stands at one end
of the porch. At the other end,
the lawn falls away to a wood where thrushes sang
through the summer evenings. But now,
on this cold morning in October,
I walk back and forth gazing out at a frieze
of bare branches. What leaves remain
hang at the ends of their twigs. The trees
are falling asleep quietly. The grass
goes on growing green without the least
foreboding.
                    I speak to my own
turbulent spirit about how Blake
wrote that eternity is in love
with the productions of time. "And so am I!"
it answers. Then tears well up
as I feel how entangled I am, and remain,
in a passion for individual things, just
as they are, the hanging leaves,
the grass, the old pear tree
grown twisted and hollow, the tin weathervane
on the barn – a galloping horse – the friends
who let their vulnerabilities flow
into my own, the one cow moose
who lives, I know, in the gully
at the back of these fields. Walking up and down
the length of the porch, I often imagine
that I can see her
stepping through the thicket along the streambed
in her lonely majesty, awkward and beautiful,
her great nose wrinkled up to browse,
her modest eye looking back into my own.

A Wet Evening

A wet evening.
    The clouds
        look brushed in

over the hills
    by a black brush
        on soaked paper.

Rain must
    already be falling
        on the other side

of the horizon
    where hilltops
        with a narrow band

of paleness floating
    over the blue-black
        undulation

of their crests
    outline
        a recumbent, stone

goddess
    who fell asleep
        some time ago

between the sea
    and this little, running,
        freshwater river.

Wishes

Waking before dawn, I hear
first one shot, then
three or four, and it isn't even
light yet. I think of how, at night,
the deer lie down in the big field, of their beds
in the rowen hay, the way
they turn their heads when anyone enters
their wide, starry chamber;

                     and I wish that buck

a whole skin, and no luck
to hunters.

Extrapolation

for Rabon Blake

Rabon, do you remember an exercise
we used to do in art school when we were young
called *extrapolation?* We had to look hard
at the model, and then draw the other side
of the form, the shapes
we guessed, the channel
of the spine, the blank sole of a foot
tucked up behind her; but my inner eye
always went farther, it slipped through the back wall
of the studio to places like this lane
we're standing in now, at the edge
of a steeply tilted hayfield. The lane drops away
below us to a track mowed through water meadows
toward the shadowy bank of a river, its blue-black silk
reflecting hills and clouds.
                            We can assume
wild flags growing down there in sheets
like ponds, snapping turtles
crossing the path on their slow
reptilian legs, blackbirds flying up
from cattails; while here, on the hillside,
we watch a hay-rake drawn by two black horses
pass through the thick shade of a line of maples
to the sunlit slopes beyond.
                            I reach down
and pick up a double handful of June hay
to press to my nose. Could we ever,
I wonder, have extrapolated
this whole sweet-smelling countryside
from such a twist of cut grass, its perfume
implicit in the wooded crests

of the line of hills, the southward-facing fall
of the fields? I think of the start
of our friendship, long ago, how I never guessed
the strong alliance that would last –
all this time, even the way we sometimes
know more, now, of one another's thoughts
than we *can* know, when a word in our endless, feminine,
coming-&-going conversation turns suddenly
transparent, startling us both – like the moment
when a shade flies up with a loud *whirr!*
from an attic window in a house
high up on a ridge.
                    The people
in the attic look out quickly,
and see a valley below them, the shapes
of its gullies and dark woods, the river that flows
down the middle in a long channel of light.

Under the Rosemary

for Gioia Timpanelli

After all this time,
it's hard to tell about the side
of the mountain. New people have the house now
and I hear they've put a tiled roof on it
and cut down some trees.
                              Meanwhile,
the grownup children living here and there
seem to be trying to reassemble
their lost world. They inhabit brushy hills,
or other lonely mountainsides, or they stay
at the edge of towns among shacks
and sunflowers, living a life at once
rackety and inspired.
                         I wonder
if we ever find our way back together
to the old house at night, emerging in our dreams
from these separate lives, stepping past
the little bantams still pecking
among the layered oak leaves, going in
at the glass door with its many leaded panes,
one of them cracked. Do we walk
through those spacious, shabby rooms – no doubt
in deep disorder – do the four children climb
on the shingles, or drop to white Pompey's back
from the green shadow of the grapes,
high on their trellis?
                         Is there a father
who walks out to his study after dark? Are there still
the many cats and dogs, the horses
and goats, do rattlesnakes curl up
under the tall herbs by the gate, do deer
thread through the oak grove below?

                                        Is there a mother
in the big bed on a rainy winter morning
who gathers them all around her
like a tattered hen clucking
to its chicks? She picks up her book
and reads aloud about a shepherdess
who once pulled up a great rosemary bush
and found carved steps underneath it
that led down into the earth, and shone
with the light of another world
streaming upward.

The Day's One Page

Squeezing garlic through the press,
I see the fragments fall with a small splash
into the warm water in the dog's dish

and disperse. I add vitamins and beef,
and the dog eyes me
as if to say, Let's pay attention here,

let's not leave anything out!
Then, while she eats, the clouds
all around the western horizon

swim off like slate-blue fish
at the bottom of a primrose ocean
and I sit down at the table

to write the day's one page
in my diary. I consider
the old dog, the clouds, the burnished sea

in the sky, this day
that has just gone by, a day at once
valuable and ordinary, a day

that is already forgetting itself
as my hand reaches out
to close around the pen.

Runes

Trifling, I ask the runes
what will happen, and my fingers close
on one that means either a gift of God
or human love.
                    Take your choice –
but isn't it always difficult to know
where we are, and who
we ever were? My eldest child,
now a mysterious, grown-up woman visitor
wearing a purple tee shirt with a leaping fish
over the heart, sits at the kitchen table
reading a book about pigs, and laughing
out loud. Moths bump at the screens
that hold the summer night out; the old dog
groans as she lies asleep
in her cavern deep among the legs
of the table.
                    When I lift my hand
as softly as I can, the tiny
perception that is a mosquito
understands the gesture, and hides itself
in the folds of the dark curtain.

Prospero's Cell

Mostly clear today,
but there are clouds at the horizon,
sagging down over the hills
like the undersides of worn-out sofas,
torn and spilling,

while I sit talking to my dead father
telling him I understand, I can see now
how it was for him, why he never once
wrote the word "daughter"

in any of his books. "I realize
you were afraid," I say, "if you'd admitted
you just had girls, that your only children
were two *daughters*, the very word
would have lifted itself off the page
to steal the pith from your arm."

And all the time
he lies under a boulder as high as my breast-bone
at the edge of the woods, a skeleton,
with one bony finger still looped
in a silver ring set with a square of old turquoise
much bluer than the sky.

Last Lines

Some people say the last line of a poem
should be a door that shuts
when you look at it one way, but then,
when you see it at another angle,
you notice that it is opening . . .
endlessly . . .
     or it can close
like the Zen master who died standing
on his head, or like Goethe
gasping out, "More light!" – the brief
encapsulation of a lifetime
in a low cry;
     or it might amble
off the page, still talking
in its usual tones, like an old woman
out in her garden on an evening
in August. "There," she says
to the ragweed she pulls up, "It's time
for *you* to come out." And she congratulates
her cat on his dead mouse, she praises
her lilies – orange-red, purple-spotted, green-starred,
their petals bending back, their faces shining –
for the efforts they are making
as they open to the tops of the tall stems
that sway in the last rays of sunlight

a foot above her head.

You Know What I Mean

You Know What I Mean

*I've dreamt in my life dreams that have stayed
with me ever after, and changed my ideas; they've
gone through and through me, like wine through
water, and altered the colour of my mind.*

Emily Brontë

The way to avoid transference
is something I often mull over. "Don't talk
so fast," I say to myself, "Don't
be *too* forthcoming; go slowly,
slowly now; you don't have to say
everything; it's possible
to interrupt this flow, to remind yourself
not, *above all*, to start discussing
the ineffable, *above all*,
in terms of beauty, invariably
followed by the words, *You know
what I mean?*
                    As in:
"I was riding a white wolf the size of a horse
through the woods at night. Ordinary wolves
ran with us, howling,
looking for those who do wrong, and I was afraid
but also elated – *You know
what I mean?*"
                    Or:
                              "My new mother-in-law,
a Chinese woman a thousand years old,
sent me an embroidered box. When I opened it,
I found two turtles inside made of turquoise enamel
on gold, inextricably
linked, their minute gold heads

bobbing as if they were alive — *You know
what I mean?"*
                    At this moment,
I look up suddenly and see the analyst's
unguarded face looking tired, indeed,
exhausted. It's impossible
not to think she must be counting the minutes, not
to come down with a bump from the ineffability
flight and ask what's really
happening here?
                    Nothing,
but human beings acting with all
their defining limits in place, or, sometimes
getting lucky, touching a power you might call
"ineffable," to pass those borders
for a moment, to reach inward
to the wholeness I assume
when I say:
                    "I went into his garden
on the edge of the mountainside. Cherry trees
hung over the valley, blooming; cedar waxwings
sat on every branch, their little topknots
lifted like crowns. When I bent
over the fountain, I saw the snowy crests
of peaks reflected all around as they leaned
inward from the edge of the sky — as if
the water in the stone basin had rounded itself
into a mirrored globe that gave me back everything
I'd ever wanted, ever lost — *You know
what I mean!"*

The Tree Ferns

When two such intellectuals unite,
beside them on the bedside table two
pairs of spectacles lie intermingled,
all legs like preying mantises, while they,
unfrocked and sportive, to the bed resort,
as pink as any pair of naked shoats.

Now all their quotes seem quite unapropos.
Where are the serious look and the black sweater?
Lady Venus standing at their feet,
is as amused with them as with all others;
her beautiful laughter, foaming up with joy,
issues kindly from their happy mouths.

When two in love become empirical,
there's no more thesis, no antithesis;
together they descend an ancient pathway
until they come into the land of dragons.
Useless to speak of them – they have got clean away;
they lie beneath the tree ferns and have no language.

Elizabeth and Sally

Black-and-white man-of-war birds soar
on impalpable drafts
and open their tails like scissors on the curves
or tense them like wishbones, till they tremble.
　　　　　– from "The Bight" by Elizabeth Bishop, 1948

Elizabeth and Sally were standing at the edge
of the bight. The water, as we all know,
was the color of a gas flame turned down
as low as possible. Both of the women
were still young, but Sally was six years behind
Elizabeth, who turned to her and said,

"I don't know if I've ever really said
anything about this before. If I seem on edge,
it might be because I've got so far behind
with sleep. I haven't slept for three nights, you know."
They were silent. The sea opened before the two young women,
a kingdom into which they could gaze down

but never particularly far down.
"I've been working on a poem," Elizabeth said,
"about the Bight. I must be one of the slowest women
alive who is writing. I find it hard to get over a certain edge.
I think this might be something you already know.
As a painter, do you sometimes feel you're behind

all the others in their work, as if you got left behind
a long time ago? And then your spirits sink down
so low that – " Sally broke in then, "Yes, I do know,

or I think I know, the feeling you mean," she said.
"In any art, it's hard to find the moving edge
and then there's the fact we both are women

who want to be taken as artists, not just women.
That's where we feel ourselves trailing behind
the men. They seem to have a natural edge.
I suppose it's inevitable for them to put us down
without even thinking about it." Elizabeth said,
"What I was doing for three nights – if you'd like to know –

was looking for one missing word. So now you know
what women do who stay up all night, at least women
who are trying to write poetry." Sally laughed, and said,
"Don't those sharks' tails make an interesting shape from behind?
I've been drawing them lately, but it's hard to get down
the full effect." The two of them looked over the edge

of the wharf. There was something else they might know,
    something behind
the things women could say. They both looked down
into moving water. Neither said anything. Then they drew
    back from the edge.

The Old Woman's Story

When my friend Clementina
was growing up in Honduras
there was an old lady in the village
who had died and come back to life.

As her body lay on the cot,
her soul got up and left it;
she walked out into the village street
which was different from usual

because, instead of ending
in a muddy track into the hills,
it now ended at the edge
of a wide, swift-flowing river.

And what was that green land
on the opposite shore
with such inviting shady trees?
Perhaps it was an island –

she couldn't quite tell –
but one thing was certain:
happiness blew toward her from that place
with a scent like vanilla flowers.

Looking anxiously around,
the old woman saw she was not alone;
other people just like her
were walking down to the bank

and as soon as each little soul
strolled uncertainly to the water's edge,
a dog would swim up
to carry it over on its back.

The dogs were as busy as sidewheelers
ferrying souls across the river.
The old woman stood watching a long while
but no canine psychopomp

hurried up to *her*,
and then – she remembered –
the kicks as she cooked the beans:
Get away, you curs, there's none for you!

So she sadly turned around,
sadly walked up the street again.
It was hard to climb back into that body,
so old and fever-wasted,

but she managed to blink her eyes,
and then she drank a little cold tea,
and after a while
she got quite well again

so that she lived on for years
telling her story over and over,
a source of deep interest to the whole village –
and a notable friend to its dogs.

To a Skylark

The fervor of images. The rising poet
on a reading tour of American colleges
spending an impulsive night in bed
with one of his listeners, a woman student
on a scholarship. She was, he felt,
lucky, really,
to get the chance, privileged,
if his poetry meant anything like as much to her
as she said it did.
                    Next morning,
after the poet had flown back to his wife
and young family, the student gave up
her scholarship, sold her books and computer,
and cleaned out her savings. She believed
every word the god had spoken, and she used
her last penny to fly off to England
after him.
                    How was it
exactly, I wonder, when she knocked
at the door of that artfully restored
stone cottage? The taxi drove away; the morning
grew very still. She heard a skylark
singing, for the first time in her life,
as she waited on the doorstep, rehearsing
her greetings. What did busy Mrs. Poet
say when she finally answered
the knock? And what did Mrs. Poet
tell her husband, later? Who paid
for the return flight of a young woman
much richer, now, in experience, if poorer
by the loss of almost everything
she owned? How long

was the incident discussed
in the poetic household?

                             But there's nothing unusual
in this story – is there? – it's been like that
forever, women immolating themselves
in the flames of art – I *suppose*
it's art – and poets
needing someone on hand to defend them
from the words they mutter when they have no idea
what they're saying, when they're overcome
by the fumes that rise from the smouldering tinder
of their anxious natures.

El Consentido

For the move back from Sonora, her husband rented
a stake-side truck, got their tables and chairs
roped together in one half, in the other
tied a bay gelding with rolling eyes
and a roman nose, a horse whose name
meant "The one who is consented to," whose anxious face
peered out over the unreeling shimmer of desert
for days.
       But at last the wife
found herself alone with the three
young children. Her husband
left them off and went back to Mexico
for awhile. It was night then. The house
they had bought seemed to reach out
and take them in, an old house
standing alone on its knoll above slopes
of slow-falling grazing land, nothing near
but two dry streambeds.
       The mother and children
walked from room to empty room, the few lamps
they had brought with them plugged in already
and shining, small islands of light
in the far reaches of shadow, as they stepped
over the smooth tiles of the unknown floor,
past halls and bedrooms, to a long dining room
where French doors led them outside again,
beneath a lattice of grapevines, onto a terrace
whose bricks slanted roughly away
under their blind soles feeling out a path
in the darkness. They could smell
a sea of aromatic brush all around them
washing upward to mountains whose black wall

bounded the drift of stars. They heard owls
hooting in the branches of the live oaks
below the bluff at their feet, and the snorting
of their horse, uneasy
in his strange paddock.
                              Everything else
hung still, open, quivering. The night air
touched cool on their cheeks, trembling slightly, brimming
with its many promises, some of them true.

Hingham

If I could only dive into the black waters that make
time up, and swim strongly enough
straight down, I could get there again,
I'm sure of it. Perhaps, on some April morning, I'll take

the same train from South Station,
past the wash-lines and small back gardens,
until I arrive at Hingham, and the walk
up the long inclination

of Fearing Road, under the new-leafed elms, to Cottage Street,
among the square eighteenth-century houses.
The spring flowers would be up. At the top
of *Ship Street formerly Fish*, I would see the sheet

of open water below, and turn in the gate
to Shipcote, toward the dark green door on the piazza, hoping,
believing, I could find them all still living
inside, unconscious in their reversed fate,

like a dream in which you never
have to understand you are dreaming.
The tall clock ticks, unmoving sunlight stretches
across the worn Persian carpets forever;

and my father is safely at work on a new book, away
in his study; and my mother is at her desk
in the corner of the long room, some small daffodils
in a green jug beside her. Glancing toward the bay,

I see far out there the three dark shoulders
of islands riding low in the blue height
of this lasting tide. In the fireplace,
the soft fire plays; it neither sparks nor smoulders.

"Mother," I try to call out then, "Mother!" but no sound
comes from my mouth, although I can hear Annie scolding
the milkman at the kitchen door. Not one of them
knows the water has risen over them, that they're drowned

under it. My mother writes on and on, happily, in her
steady hand. Pug snores in his basket at her feet.
But she doesn't look up. How could she look up —
or hear me now, or turn in her chair, or give any answer?

Ribe

Begin at the beginning
again. You find yourself in a low skiff
in the darkness, waiting until the water rises
under you. Then you feel the soft
nudge and lift; you are floating
through a forest of tall reeds
much higher than your head; paths open
where enormous swans swim out suddenly
from side channels to flap and hiss.
They seem to be looming above you, stately
and threatening, in the sulphurous light
of the full moon caught in the reeds

where it shines as if from under water.
And where am I? you ask. Outside the town
of Ribe, I think. I don't suppose
this body is really walking
from saltmarsh to street again, listening
to the bells that ring their old song
of Queen Dagmar lying in grief
on her deathbed. It must be my soul
that stands among brick pillars in the church
where the windows are set high up,
as if in a fortress, and the moon
sends her light to play illusively

through clear panes over painted saints
on the walls. The soul sees the she-dragon
impaled on Saint George's spear, his white horse
rearing up, the knight thrusting downward,
the spitted dragoness writhing,
showing two lines of pale dugs

on her underside. At the mouth
of a nearby cave, a litter of dragon cubs
peers out anxiously at their dam
in her throes. I step
past these green orphans into
the darkness behind them. I can feel

the passageway growing narrower, rock walls
encroaching on the body, bowing
the head, making the shoulders
fold forward of themselves,
but I go on inching back
through the complete blackness
on the blind wormtrack underneath
the painted mountain that seemed
no higher than . . . what? A mound,
perhaps, lower for sure
than the saint's rearing stallion. The floor
leads upward now, and my outstretched hand

finds a small, smooth world
in its grasp, the round knob
of a door that opens
with a shriek to lamplight
on a red tablecloth and floorboards
sloping like the deck
of a ship at sea. My mother
stops her pen in its traveling
as I step out into her room.
She raises her head and smiles
from the chair where she sits writing
at an inn table. Our eyes meet

with a look of recognition
and joy. It is as though she were saying,
"It's all right, you know."
I look, I look, I keep looking
as if I would never stop
gazing into her face – but I find myself
walking away down a corridor
into the narrow street, past the walls
of the small city, through the marshlands
where dun horses graze on saltgrass
and seastreams reach into their pastures

as the lonely fingers of a translated hand
might still reach out lovingly
toward an earthly hand. Swans sleep
on the incoming tide, reeds
whisper and whisper like people
who can never quite say what they wish
they could; the current whispers
along the sides of the narrow skiff
that seems to be floating through and on
nothing but the strange saffron light
of the round moon to begin once more
at the beginning.

Leaving

My father told my mother, and she told me
that I didn't have to go to boarding school
until I was thirteen. I didn't think
much about it, I understood
there was no choice. Our father often reminded us
that in England children went off to school
at seven or eight.
                        That September
my mother bought me a gray wool skirt
at Peck & Peck's, and a gray wool jacket
at Best's, to wear on the trip. They weren't quite
the *same* gray; neither she nor I
knew much about clothes.
                        I put them on
and climbed into an old railroad car
with worn plush seats that smelled of steam
and dust. Just before the train started,
my mother hugged me hard and pressed a book
into my hands, a thick, dark blue one,
The Oxford Book of English Verse. All the way
through western Massachusetts and on
into upper New York State, I sat there
looking out the window and turning
the many pages of my book
over and over, strong, thin pages
with gilded edges, catching a line
here and a line there, a clamber
of rocky hillside here, a shallow,
brown river there, running fast
among tall elms with sand bars rising
in long, low islands only inches above
the braided surface *to whose falls
melodious birds sang madrigals.*

"In the Realm of the Mothers"

for Elizabeth Coatsworth Barnes

When I was twenty-three, I got up in the morning
peculiarly dizzy, and thought, "I can't be
pregnant, I'm not educated, I've never even
learned German!"
                But I was.
In the hospital I watched my roommate
unwrap her child and count his fingers and toes
so I unwrapped my own child, and counted
her fingers and toes. Then what? The tiny thing
lay wrapped again in her receiving blanket,
like a candy baby. She had a name
already, "Elizabeth," taken from my mother
and great-grandmother, and many more women
in a file behind them that receded
slowly backward into the blue
of time, their heavily-folded skirts
hanging like silent bells. The baby
slept, and I tentatively
sketched the crushed-looking planes
of her bruised new face, the stripes
of her pink blanket. While I gazed at her,
her cells were dividing invisibly, she was growing
steadily forward. She smelled of clean cotton, talcum,
and her own new flesh; I longed to sniff her
all over, like a dog with its puppy.
                      The nurse,
starched and crackling, guided my nipple
into that weak mouth whose first sips
encouraged the secret mind of the breasts
to give more, make more, teach me from inside
a new feeling that melted through me and startled me

like a shot of whiskey. I looked up
from the wrinkled infant face, and my eyes wandered
past florists' carnations, through the plate glass window,
and on over lined-up roofs, to rest
on a frieze of bare blue mountains receding
into the summer sky, fold
after unfathomable fold.

A Wedding

for Carol Rohl and Gordon Bok

If love is the poem of our youth, written
in mousetracks through new snow, in the curved lip
of drifts that mean to stay awhile, the whirling
of snow devils on the hills, the wings
of a flock of snow buntings
turning together in the midst of their flight
with the sudden flash of a shared thought, the air
two people begin humming at the same
exact moment – they catch
each other's eye – they smile –

                           then time

is a song we come to
later, the snow melting
from below, invisibly, everything changing
to damp earth underfoot and a trembling screen
of new leaves overhead, the harbor open
at last, the sails going up –
rattle, rattle! – the wind rising, the tune in our mouths
stronger now, and sweeter
than ever before.

Other Nations

for Maxine Kumin

I used to think women who talked baby talk
to their animals were the rock bottom. Now I'm not
so sure. Now I open my mouth
and hear, coming out of it, "Is you
a good, *good* dog?" – words that are falling
in their light, descending order to two pricked ears,
a hairy face, a glowing eye, an unbroken
concentration on the excellent, bone-shaped dog biscuit
I'm holding up, increasing our pleasure
with some slight, prolonging chitchat.

                                 My neighbor Zoë,
at twelve, cries to her cat, "Oh, dearest, darlingest
Wooshiekins!" as she presses extravagant kisses
on the round head of a pale, torpid marmalade
who doesn't seem to mind (but her silent father
gets up and leaves the room).

                          "They are other nations,"
my own father wrote, "caught with ourselves
in the net of life and time." Of course, he meant
the wild ones, but our household allies, too,
link us to a greater world. We wish
we could speak their languages; and, meanwhile,
they learn ours.

                  When the rein snaps
while I'm driving home in the buggy, with Blackberry
trotting hard, grabbing the bit, through the rush
of a blustery March day, I don't start hauling
on the other rein and risk tipping us over
or starting a runaway; I call to him loudly,
"Wa-alk … wa-alk …" – and after he does that
he hears me say, "Whoa!" – and does that.

So how can I ever
praise that huge person enough, those twelve hundred pounds
of best behavior who may just have saved
my life? I get out and tie the ends
of the parted rein as he rolls
his questioning eye, and I pat
his strong, damp neck, repeating, over and over,
without thought, a mantra of gratitude to gods
and animals. "Thank you," I say, "thank you,
thank you, kind fate, thank you, my good, *good* friend!"

Sisters: The Point of a Pin

"What did you have for breakfast?" I ask
on the long distance line, "Did you remember
to eat?" "Oh, yes," you tell me, "I had a bottle
of champagne for my breakfast, and I want you
to talk French now."
                                        So we speak awhile
about the houses of our childhood, arguing – and laughing –
over where the chairs and tables stood, how many blue deer
ran on our mother's bed curtains. Then you read a note
from one of your daughters. "She ends," you say suspiciously,
"with 'God bless you.' Do you think that means
she loves me? And on the flap of the envelope
she writes, 'I have kissed the note here,
and another kiss *here*, both as dry and chaste
as spider bites.' Do you really think
she loves me?"
                                "Yes," I say,
"She's a loving girl, she's a lot like our mother."
"No," you answer fiercely, "She is no far lake
among icy white waterfalls; *no one*
is like our mother!" I think of our mother, someone
I've never connected with ice. "To be clean glass,"
says a poem of hers, "to be clear water,
that is beautiful, my daughter."
                                                "Mousie," I say,
"our mother wouldn't want her children
to leave strife behind them. Why don't you make
a fair will?" You giggle your feathery giggle,
as spontaneous as air. "I dreamed I had died
already," you tell me, "and I was lying
on a cloud, looking down at all my children
fighting over my stuff. I laughed so hard,
I almost fell off the cloud."

Two long operations
survived, the future uncertain, but you never speak
of fear. If you mention your troubles, it's as though
they were just gnats. You go right on giving
your wild presents, a heavy gold bracelet
to the hotel maid – "Do you think
she'll like it?" – and a large TV set
to your former husband's sister
when she invites you to dinner.
                              Oh, world of objects,
all shining in their own radiance! "Poor boy," you say,
speaking of your new son-in-law, "he can only afford
to give her diamonds no bigger
than the head of a pin – no, no, I mean
the *point* of a pin!"

Knowing the Goddess Epona

Knowing the Goddess Epona

Epona, I love you,
but it's hard to know who you are. Sometimes
you're a white mare, and sometimes
a woman riding a white mare
with a foal at foot. At other times
you're a goddess who sits in the horse lot
holding a lapful of barley. Seven horses
crowd around you, but politely, no kicking
or squealing where *you* are.
                              Often
you carry bread or fruit. In your pocket
there's a key, but no one can tell me
whether it opens the stable door
or the locks of the sky.
                         When I come closer
you shimmer and change, you are suddenly
three shining girls, or else
three springs welling from stone, one called
Meditation and the other two
Inspiration and *Memory*. Their white threads
gleam as they braid themselves together
down the dark rockface before they hurry off
in a small stream that talks softly
to the hillside, to the roots
of the listening oaks, to the sparrows
in the branches, to the goats
browsing below, to the old woman
who has fallen asleep in the shade, her basket of cresses
half-full beside her.

To the Goddess Epona on a Snowy March Day

Epona, if you came here today,
riding your white mare
over these long slopes of snow,
would I even be able
to see you?

Perhaps I would see the raven
who sometimes flies with you, or the dog
who often follows.

The sky would be white,
the way it is now, and the jays would still squawk
in the leafless sumacs. You would sit sideways
on the mare's back, holding your basket

of barley in your lap, your wreath of bread
in one hand, promising that the snow
won't cover the fields forever, that some morning,
quite soon, we'll see the earth
naked again under the tall sun, and all her bare ground
blushing green.

Conversation

"Well, I will, and I won't, and I don't know
  what I will do at all," said the car,
  striking a ridge of ice in the road, and careening
  from edge to edge.
                   I said,
"We're going off – no, maybe
  we're coming back – no, no,
  we're going over the brink – "
                       and the car
leapt downward, like a seal diving
from a cliff ledge into a foaming wave, through the long,
steep slope of snow and air, saying, "Oh –
oh – oh – "
            and I said, "Oh –
oh – " and then I said, "The snow
at the bottom will stop us," and the car and I
both said, "*Ohhhhh!*" as it rolled itself
right over, fast.
             I didn't know
what had happened, only that I was flung hard
all around, and then it was suddenly
still again, and the car stopped,
upright on its four black tires. There was no one
in sight, but I could hear chickadees
calling, "Fee-bee, fee-bee,"
from the sunlit woods behind us. The spent car
stood steaming like a horse, and none of my bones
was broken.

Trotsky Ghazals

Once you're old, you wonder, whenever you get sick,
if maybe this time you're actually for it.

My little cat lies on the bolster behind my head;
in the darkness the whole bed thrums with her long purr.

Down in the swamp the grass-grown wood roads, half-lost,
cross and twist and cross again like my thoughts at two in the
morning.

Trotsky wrote that, of all the things that happen to a person,
the most surprising is old age.

Some rocks in our village sandpit date from the time when blue-
green
   algae
were the only living beings, breathing out for billions of years
the oxygen which has made everything possible.

With their leaves of commingled vines, their scarlet made of
many
   different reds,
after the first frost, the blueberry fields shout on the hillside.

"Kate!" you cried out in our moonlit bed long ago. It was the
old,
   old bliss;
it just was; and I don't care how misleading it was.

Ver

Although it's still snowy outside,
the little pomegranate tree planted
in a pot on the windowsill
lifts her leaves to the sun, holding them up

for the light to pass through.
When you look carefully, you think you can see
the motion of her slow dance, choreographed
to the time trees take. And she has put out

four fierce, orange-red blossoms,
long tubes, each ending in a frill
of petticoats, like the skirts
of a Spanish dancer, a passionate woman

who sings, almost shouting, *My body is so full
of songs that it's like a wasps' nest.
They push one another out
to see who will come first!*

The End of March

Still frozen under the skin, seeming to hold
no promise of life, this dead body of winter
beginning to turn back into the living body of April
changes slowly. It isn't easy
to transform oneself, and it's still so cold,
anyway, that nothing appears
to happen. But pussy willows
have emerged, flickering with light
in the raw wind, and buds thicken
the bare apple twigs. I can hardly imagine
how it will be in another two months
when they flower, spreading out their immoderate
white petals, when the long battle
between winter and life will be over
for one more year, and we will all be living
on the perfume of blossoming apple trees
and opening lilacs, drawing in immortality
with every breath – for who can believe in dying
while he pushes his face into the breast
of a flowering tree?
                        Chives
strive upward now; robins pipe; the old dog
lies in the sun with her eyes shining
like translucent stones. The lines of snow
that stripe the brown fields are melting invisibly
from underneath, and I find myself
buying many small packets at the grocery
that hiss or sigh as the seeds inside them
shift.

My thoughts circle back
to a young medical student who said she was frightened,
when her teacher warned his first-year class
they would all have nightmares, sooner or later,
about the dissecting room; but, when a cadaver
appeared in one of her dreams, she only found herself
sitting beside it, holding its cold hand
comfortingly, as any doctor
might hold the hand of any patient
through a difficult procedure.

Easter Morning

A rainy Easter morning, clouds that feather
the line of the hills, everyone saying

how gloomy it is. And it's true, it's been raining
on and off for days, but the lame farmer I meet

hobbling out of church tells me we need
every drop; no matter how caught up

the average may be, the soil is still dry
from last year, lovely on top

with its first greenness, but parched
underneath. At home, I turn on the tap

and think of the spring welling up
in the woods, the place my water

comes from. My life
has been so lucky, years

of blessings falling from the sky
as rain and rising from the ground

as green stalks underfoot, and now, still,
almost every evening the deer

step over the rim of the slope
to graze in the April field, eager

for the fresh grass, but watchful, too,
flicking their tails and stamping their small hoofs.

A Party

My neighbor who hates everyone
doesn't hate the space around his trailer.
I hear his lawn tractor start up
on this late May afternoon
and I know he is riding back and forth, peacefully
beheading the grasses, drinking whiskey from his flask,
making circles around the blooming apple trees
as he dreams about whom he could sue, and for what.

Even in repose, his face
is as fierce as the face of a wild boar.
The small eyes are hot. Above him,
the old trees sway their blossoms,
white and pink, against the clear sky.

When he first moved here
he tried to make a fresh start;
he drank less, he made an effort to be civil.
Once, while he was still speaking to us,
he said he thought he'd give a garden party
every year when the apple trees were in bloom.

Aye Waukin', O!

1.

My neighbor comes in,
bringing small daffodils, the sort
you could fall in love with, the way a girl
caught sight of another world
through the opening center of a jonquil, a boy
drooped so long over the reflection
of his face, that his arms –
at last! at last! – turned into thin leaves,
his hair to petals.

2.

The loggers up the ridge,
who are clearing the top of the slope
to nothing at all, drive their big loads
too fast down this small road;
we have to watch how their trucks
sway, and how the bodies of the trees
are leaving us.
                    Someone
has cut the hoses on their skidders
several times.

3.

Unable to sleep, I lie thinking
of my lost books, the old life, the house,
surrounded by brush with troops of deer
streaming through it, where the children shouted
outside in the garden, and I could look up
anything I wanted.
                    I have to remind myself
that Paradise is always,
and is now.

4.

I never get used to it, the sight of the moon's
big belly growing eastward, pregnant
only with light, and the reflection
that answers from the snow
on the open fields.

           At night, I wander
like a moth through my darkened house
with a moth's joy, a moth's longing
for the blue fire all around.

Cabin Tankas

for Elizabeth Tibbetts

The cabin beside the rocks —
    sand dollars and shells
lined up on the windowsill
    and the sea outside
pouring up its stony shelf
in a long rush of moonlight.

                Another thing I always
                    like about cabins —
                the flotsam that washes up
                    over the years there:
                driftwood and shells, the odd plates
                from the shelves of lost pantries.

This pitcher on the table
    filled with the flowers
of late summer — goldenrod,
    black-eyed Susans, and
a few bachelor's buttons —
looks out to sea all day long.

                Eating dinner here means these
                    lobsters as red as
                fire engines, and red wine
                    from the south of France
                to drink with them. We toast our
                hopes, and then the moonlit waves.

Family identity
    is never stronger
than in a seaside cabin
    full of old books, charts,
plates, shells, and drawings by the
long ago grownup children.

        You say you would like to die
           here at this window,
        looking out at the harbor
           of Spruce Head Island,
        hearing to the last the waves,
        the gulls, and the off-shore wind.

Sometimes

at night, as I drive up
the dark field-track,
I see,
suddenly,
something so
small in the headlights, so
distant, a delicate, gray
shape that bounds off
toward the drop of the gully;
                              and then
there's another . . . and another . . . and
then it's the three does pausing
to look back as they reach
the stone wall,
                  and it's
myself caught in the flash
of their eyes, the course
of six gentle, luminous, green
planets under the wide field
of summer stars.

Early Summer

I

In the middle of June the hot weather comes in suddenly, and all the lilacs leap into their fullest bloom. It is the end of spring. I meet Denise walking up her steps, her arms filled with deep lavender blossoms, as many as she can hold. "I like to have them in every room," she says, "I want to enjoy them while they're here."

"Do you fray their stems," I ask her, "Do you hit them with a hammer the way people say we're supposed to?"

"No," she says, "I can't."

That night a summer rain falls. I drive out to do an errand at midnight, and the wet tar shines like black glass in the car's headlights. The tall, dark-purple lilacs at the edges of the old pasture seem to lean over the road to see the reflections of their new blossoms. My headlights sweep through their leaves in unpredictable scrims of light.

II

When I was a young mother, far from here, I sometimes rode my horse alone in the mountains all day. I passed those long hours in a kind of solitary ecstasy, gazing at blue peaks, at the purple spires of penstemon, at the gray deer running off like spirits among the oak trunks. But the landscape was only a painted box to hold my real happiness, the inner joy I wasn't even thinking about, that I could hardly have put into words.

And inside *that*?

Trash Roses

Wind stirs the high grass; swallows dip low in the light summer rain. Drifts of buttercups run through the water meadows, and a few of the last blue flags are still opening. Two white horses toss their heads as they graze, their long tails fanning out like fringed silk.

The whole valley moves as if it were alive. The edges of the leafy willow branches, picked out with pale green, reflect the storm light; like the horses' white tails, they never stop flickering. Above the trees, torn rain clouds blow fast in front of blue-gray cumulus. You can't see the river behind its fringe of woods, but you can feel its presence, wide and dark, flowing strongly and almost silently.

Robins sing their rain song.

Gone-wild white roses, escaped polyanthas, bloom all around, in thickets beside the dirt road, in high clumps on the slopes of the pasture. On my way here, I noticed their sprays, like miniature drinking swans, bending down to a pool, the tiny crowded faces of the flowers drooping into the black water. They are trash roses, hard to root out, thorny determined weeds that make a lot of trouble for farmers. Today the moist air is filled with their scent. It's like breathing perfume to breathe that air; I take it in in great thirsty snuffs; I can't get enough; I've never smelled anything so heart-breakingly sweet. I drove here over thirty-seven miles of back roads, drinking in that scent the whole time. It was there all the way, but it's strongest here in the damp river valley.

Oh, roses, I think, Oh, precious earth! What is more loving than summer, more generous than this momentariness, this unspoken assent?

A Summer Night

A summer night. The moon's face,
almost full now, comes and goes
through clouds. I can't see
any stars, but a late firefly
still flicks his green lamp on and off
by the fence.
                    In this light
that is more illusion
than light, I think of things
I can't make out: milkweed opening
its millions of flowerets, their heavy heads
smelling like dark honey in the night's
darkness; day lilies
crowding the ditch, their blossoms
closed tight; birds asleep with their small legs
locked on twigs; deer stealing
into the uncut hay; and the young bay mare
kneeling down in the pasture, composing herself
to rest, as rounded and strong
as a meant prayer.

Wanting to See a Moose

When I am full
of some transporting emotion,
what I see is that ordinary things
are all extraordinary. But
it's like gathered dew
on a blade of grass, it falls off
or dries up, and I can't hang on
to the feeling. In no time
I'm back asking the fates
to let me see a moose
as I drive my car through the marsh – and not
attending to the gathering darkness
of evening, the cloudy light
that lingers, the reeds, the ducks,
the black, still water opening
so silently
beyond the causeway.

Twentieth-Century Pleasures

A visiting Russian poet climbed into the cart beside me
and said, "Fuck the twentieth century,
huh, Kate?" He's right. We all find
our escape routes. What I like
is driving my small cart into the woods
on a summer evening when thrushes are singing
in the old pine trees beside the lake.
Pad, pad, go the horse's hooves
on pine needles and grass; the birds' slow music
floats out over the cove; an answer returns
from the opposite shore.
                         It was like this
when I was a child, and in some ways
it still is, in others
it's more a matter of acid rainfall reports
in the daily paper. Are they what comes
to mind when you half-wake before dawn
to the touch of rain on the roof –
at last! – the slow brushing
of the light drops, the sigh
of the southwest wind that slants them
across your shingles?
                  Who *could* think
of acidification
at that moment, who could linger
murmuring, "Three-point-seven, I'll bet,"
while he lets the sounds of rain
run into his dreams, his pores,
his open limbs, helpless in sleep, the very bones
inside them?
                No one. All we can say
is what the world says plainly

and innocently around us, "*Rain,*
rain, rain . . ." not mourning –
for once – her induced fevers, the wounds
festering in the body which still clasps us
with lingering affection, no more able
to take in grief than a child can ride
the down-rush of the swing while he rises
into heady air, than a bird can migrate
north while it flies south, than you,
or I, or anyone,
can see both sides at once
of the coin that Fortune spins through infinite space
from her fine, untroubled fingers.

Hunting Season

for Virginia S. Brun

At gray dawn, I wake
to a long, broken rhythm of shots, an irregular
popping noise. Hunting season. You can't
ignore it, pickup trucks parked close
the length of the ridge, hunters
striding up the fields together,
their guns on their shoulders. Orange streamers
flutter on fence wires, a dead buck,
hoisted in the tagging scale by the store,
hangs his branchy head.

                My friend Sally,
at eighty-three, walks out in her woods
wearing an orange plastic vest. Her dog
wears one too. "We're just as orange
as they are," she says to me,
over a cup of tea, "and, besides,
at my age, what would it matter?"

                        Later,
as I drive home in the dark, my headlights sweeping
the tunnel of tree trunks, two does
bound across the road, still frightened
hours after sunset. *May you be lucky,*
beautiful ones. On the spine of the ridge,
the trees fall away and I suddenly see the moon,
two days from the full, looking down, her head
tilted toward her invisible
left shoulder. She is wearing
a smile made from her mountains
and valleys, the hard bedrock
of the real, a sad smile
that lends an appearance of pity
to her radiant face.

New Year, 2000

I have been fanciful and unwise,
a drunkard of the printed word.
Now I must give away half my books
or I won't be able to walk into the kitchen
at all.
      The New Year
has come, it's time now
to clear things up around here, inside
and out. Last night
I swept the old year out at the back door
(with thanks) and welcomed
the new year in at the front door
(with wishes).
        New Year, New Year,
coming in from the frosty darkness,
with Orion over your shoulder, my wish
is to live at peace
with my heart, my house – groaning with books,
though it still is – with my friends,
with my children wherever
they happen to be, with my neighbors,
with the cat on the bed,
with the stars
dancing their slow round
over the ridge pole, with the deer
outside in the snowy thicket, with the earth
under the snow, even with the times
that taste so metallic in my mouth – and with everyone else
who is grieving in this world – and with everyone else
who is wishing, too.

Why Do You Ask?

Why Do You Ask?

for Donald Hall

I can't make
    any story
        about my life

tonight. The house
    is like an overturned
        wastebasket;

the radio
    is predicting
        more snow.

I ask my dog
    to tell me
        a story, and she

never hesitates.
    "Once upon
        a time," she says,

"a woman lived
    with a simply
        wonderful dog..." and

she stops talking.
    "Is that all?"
        I ask her.

"Yes," she says,
    "Why do you ask?
        Isn't it enough?"

Restaurant Ghazal

A knifeblade of sunlight cuts across the shadowed hillside,
and the yellow crests of the poplars stretch up eagerly.

The late fall afternoon is heart-rending,
its maple leaves gone, its brown oak leaves incandescent.

By the restaurant window, a man and woman sit talking about education
the whole afternoon. They are telling each other their lives.

Now even the battered lugger at the wharf is in shadow
but the tops of her two masts still pierce the last slant of light.

Taking my check, the cashier says, "Mrs. Barnes, may I have
     your number?"
I don't say it's unlisted, I just make one up for her.

Thirteen Ways of Looking at a Black Horse

I.

A black horse stands in the falling snow
until it lies on him like a white blanket. It looks
as though he is carrying a piece of the sky.

2.

At this very minute, King Arthur and all his knights
are sleeping in the darkness of a cavern
that runs back through limestone schist for miles
under the Eildon Hills.
                              Their black horses,
saddled and shod, stand sleeping
beside them.

3.

The north wind whistles outside the barn
on winter nights, but the big stall
is warm, with its straw
piled deep, and a black horse
folded down in it like an iron lamb
                              on a kitchen shelf.

4.

Then, one morning, the apple trees
wake up nubbled with buds, and the brown fields
begin turning greener minute
by minute.
          A black horse
dances up and down the pasture.

5.

For five years of war, the black horses
of the Household Cavalry stayed in London
among falling bombs. When peace came
they were trucked into the country and turned out
in a field, soft earth under their feet,
fresh grass. It was like a flock
of blackbirds someone has thrown
a stone into, an explosion
of black horses flying off
in every direction, squeals, kicks, leaps — mad joy
that could not be contained.

6.

In May, the pear tree
formed an arch of white blossoms
to amuse the bees
and to make a light shade
for the back of the black horse
dozing under it.

7.

Warm light
on the black horse's back flashes
a grackle sheen, while his quarters,
as full as grapes, round down
in blue shadows.

8.

A prince stepped into a forbidden tower
hesitantly. It was silent there. Dust gathered
thick on the floor, or danced

in the narrow shaft of light falling
from a shot-window; the rest of the room
stayed in shadow. Spiderwebs
linked the gilt candlesticks, the damascened steel
of hanging armor, the swords and lances, all carrying
spells inscribed in letters like snakes
of molten gold that undulated
down the fierce blades.
                              In one corner
lay a living horse, blacker
than the eye of the sun. It lifted its head
and looked across at the boy. "Ah!"
said its brilliant glance, "It is you, you have come.
At last."

9.
"Try it," says the Barra grandfather, "read my riddle.
A black horse and a dun race together
at the tide-line, hoofprints meeting
hoofprints. Give up? Then I'll tell you:
the dun horse is water,
but the black horse is the west wind, it runs the faster."

10.
At the top of the ridge, it's sky and blue hills
all around, blueberries
underneath, the black horse
resting between the shafts
of his blue cart, panting, and the cart
rocking like a skiff on the quick waves
of his breath.

11.

Given one more impossible task, a castle
to build overnight, or a princess
to fetch from Land-under-waves, the orphaned prince
went out and leaned his elbow
on his black horse's mane. He sighed.
"Sigh of a king's son under spells! – "
said the little horse, "But have no care;
we shall do the thing that is set before us."

12.

In late summer, the afternoon wind
blows with a sound like the barn door
rolling open. The old black horse
lifts his head from the pasture trough, letting the water
fall from his washed mouth.

13.

I dreamed a great box
in a cellar, and inside that
a smaller box, and in that
a smaller one yet, and so forth, and I
climbed into all of them, carefully, one
after another – until I crept
into the smallest box
of all, with a very small door
in one wall, which I opened
and found myself outside on the suddenly
greenest grass I had ever seen, the greenest
green there never was.
                              Black horses
were running and playing in it.

94

Rocking

Oh, rocking, that rocking motion – what a deep thing rocking is, how comforting! The unborn child rocks in the womb, the baby in its mother's arms. The fisherman rocks in his boat, the summer boarder in her green-painted rocking chair on the inn porch. The praying Hassid rocks as he reaches toward God, the lovers rock on their bed – and laugh, I hope! – the hurt child rocks as he sucks his burnt finger, the old woman in her wheelchair rocks back and forth as she sits speechless in the corridor of the nursing home.

The poet finds himself rocking at his desk as he concentrates – Come, words! – and I rock as I remember cantering my bay gelding along the side of a canyon by the light of a full moon. The narrow stream glinted far below me, the black boughs of the live-oaks met over my head, the horse rocked along the slight path, invisible in the shadow. Suspended in the rhythm of his light, easy bounding, I understood that he wasn't really moving at all, I knew that the Holy Earth Herself was unrolling under his hooves.

The Island of Honey

On the kitchen counter, there is a blue chafing dish full of water, with a square glass jar of honey standing in it. The ants can't get to the jar. They think about it all day, and dream of it all night; they call it "The Island of Honey."

At bed-time, the ants hum lullabies to their children about the water lapping at the shores of the island. During the day, they sing tragic ballads of adventurers who drowned trying to reach its glassy cliffs. Emmet Anthole, the best known contemporary ant artist, has painted canvas after canvas obsessively repeating the island image; and Defourmis, their great composer, wrote a harp-like piano étude they all love, "L'Île de Miel."

To the ants, The Island of Honey represents the transcendent, the numinous, the "beyond." They believe it is the source of four invisible rivers of nectar which flow out unseen to sweeten the antish creation. Once, they say, their forefathers lived in that paradise of sticky, delicious light; but, owing to an unfortunate misunderstanding, they had to leave.

All ants, even the most severely rational, expect to return to the island at the end of their lives – or of the world – they are not quite clear which. And they are not entirely clear, either, about how that will happen, whether they will travel in their present carapaces, or as disembodied souls.

When I crush an ant under my thumb on the breadboard, there is no sound; but the other ants, far off down the counter, scurry away. Do they hear screams too delicate to penetrate my giant eardrums? Does the doomed ant cry out, even as he perishes, "Oh, my far island, my blessed Island of Honey – "?

Lines Beginning with an Anacreontic Fragment

For she seems to hear
if one only wishes to speak, sang
an ancient Greek, a young man,
garlanded at the *symposion*, saluting
the dancer at whose feet he had just tossed
a coin for luck; and I,
divided by twenty-five hundred years
from his brown, prow-like face, the fennel leaves
drooping across his brow, the dark-red wine
splashing in his cup as he gestured
freely, grandly – I looked
over his shoulder, waiting for the wine
to be drunk, for the painting
at the bottom of the cup to show
itself; the god
sailing through commingled sea and sky,
alone, with seven dolphins
leaping around him, his forehead
crowned by upright leaves, his body wrapped
in a mantle of stars, his mast entwined
by two tall, interlacing vines.
                            But why
do seven clusters of black grapes hang down
so heavily over his sacred head
like portents from dancing Fate, like promises
of what will be torn, what
will be crushed, what will seem
to perish awhile, what will flow out,
what will work in darkness, what will come to life
once more in the hand on the strings, in the music
rising strong in the young man's mouth?

Miklós Radnóti, 1909–1944

Separated from her, he saw her blue eyes in the sky,
his young wife whom he called
"beautiful as light, beautiful as shadow."
Meanwhile, the forced march, men pissing blood,
the last beaten to death – and he among them,
one more dead man tumbled
into the common pit.
                    When his wife got there,
two years later, to identify the body,
she found a notebook still in his trenchcoat pocket,
the poems inside it growing smaller and smaller
as his strength gave way. Almost
at the end, he told about watching sheep
step into shallow water
by a lakeshore. "The rippled flock,"
he wrote, "bends to the clouds and drinks."

The Harrier

for Baron Wormser

The mist disperses and lifts from the field
in the whitest feathers, feathers dropped, perhaps,
from the harrier quartering
over the brown grass, which already
is beginning to green. I think
about angels, I wonder
if *they* ever catch mice? Everything
is here to accept this morning, to take in,
to applaud: the hawk's wide, predatory
circles, sunlight coming and going, cloud shadows
constantly shifting, a toss of rain, and then
the line of bare poplars standing ghostly
under the slope in a streak
of sudden light (but we know
there are buds on those pale twigs) and the veils
of moisture that hang in the air,
visible . . . invisible . . . making the hills soft,
and distant, and mildly blue, and changeable,
like the breath in my body, in
and then out . . . in and then out . . .
as long as it will.

Asters

for Christie Dennis

Mackerel clouds in a clear sky, no promise
of the rain we need, only this late summer day;
pickerel weed in the marsh stream,
yellow water lilies standing up
like lotuses above reflected clouds
on the still surface, the soft beat
of the mare's hoofs as we drive the small cart
along the causeway, talking
among dragonflies.
                            Behind us,
the marsh closes in a distant wall
of cedars marking the edge of a boggy wood
where moose tread out their circling paths
deep in the interwoven shadow
of many branches.
                            We sing
as we trot slowly along, *Adieu,*
Sweet Amaryllis; *Speed, Bonnie Boat*; we talk —
two women — about our loves
and marriages, the difficult progression
to a kind of knowledge, the learning
to rejoice, at last, in what is. "I hold
to the faith," you say, "that God
sees through my separateness."

It is hard
to understand, to see that all my old dreams
have contracted just
into this, an August afternoon, the glint
of pale blue chicory in the ditch, touch-me-not
hanging orange above it, asters
reaching across the tangle of tired leaves –
dry, darkened, thickly grown, turning brittle –
like drifts of light beside the road, stitches
on a rough, unrolling cloth, as white and open
as the stars they are.

Potnia: The Lady of the Labyrinth

Another gray morning. I wander
through my neglected house, papers
and books stacked two feet deep on every table

and chair. Without thought, I fall
into five thick, dark-blue volumes
on the archaeology of Knossos and return,

as if in a dream, to that Edwardian
dream-kingdom, the carefully rebuilt
stairs and porticos, the red pillars, the griffins

and dolphins, stalks of lilies, open-breasted
court ladies, a world we can't help
hoping was possible, its unwarlike King

reflected in the rock crystal eyes
of a black serpentine bull's head, round curls
incised on the brow echoing the spiral

borders that coil and uncoil across the walls
of the painted palace. But, listen,
can you hear roars from the labyrinth,

after four thousand years? Were animals
torn apart there and their living flesh
devoured? Are the white feet

circling the mosaic pattern of the dance floor
spattered with blood? Have the bones
of children been uncovered in the sanctuary,

chipped by priests' knives? What ogres
stand in the darkness below us, holding up
on their strong arms the many-tiered

edifice, the sacrament, the poet's mind, even
this second in which my eye
turns so eagerly to watch a flock of doves

seething over corn on the lawn? Their gray feathers
are iridescent; their wings lift,
here and there, as if an invisible goddess

moved among them, as if her moonlike glare
still burned in the shocked air, as if the world
were being born right now and hadn't even

begun to breathe.

"*The Rhetoric of Fiction*"

Chapter One: The Lion

for Marion Stocking

On a warm April evening
when I was nineteen,
a young man and woman
were walking under the oak trees,
and he was saying
the things his gonads suggested,
and she was thinking
that an angel visiting earth would talk
exactly like him.
Then he brought out a bottle
of sweet, cheap muscatel,
as yellow as a yellow cat,
and they sat down to drink it
in the fresh grass by the stream.

*He that would eat the fruit
must climb the tree.* When they got up
to leave, he had had what he said
he wanted; but perhaps it wasn't
all he wanted. He did want
what he got, and she did want
to be his, forever, but each of them
also wished the other's wish
unknowingly –
                    and this collusion
was not at all visible to them
then.

An owl, further up the canyon,
shrieked among the leaves,
and the blood on the grass
told its old story.

She couldn't stop to listen.
She was much too busy holding on
to a strong lion whose glittering mane
would cover her, and keep her
shining with reflected gold
forever.
        How long
is forever? It's not
forever. Next year
there's a flood, the stream changes
its course, willows and cottonwoods
spring up, new lilies
bloom like live coals
in the leaf shadow of new banks.
The deer make fresh paths.
We forget the old channel.

But she would remember the dusk
turning into darkness, the slow stars
coming out, the green, damp smell
of the bushes, the sound of running water;
and she would not forget the wonder –
for how could she have guessed it,
that this world of clay could contain
the gold, the fire, the burning, starry animal?

Chapter Two: Bodies

We hear it, don't we, the scrape and slide
of the fingers on the guitar,
the in-drawn breath in the mouth of the flute,
the concert pianist
humming to himself, the dancer's feet
giving a good thump as she comes back to earth?

Chapter Three: The Leaves

In the San Gabriel hills, it's always summer
because the leaves are never off the trees.
Lovers there lie twined under the live-oaks,
music plays in the winter stream beds.
New leaves on the sycamores, like small, green hands,
each hold a patch of cliff or a minute piece
of the sky.
        I went there once. The mountains
hovered on the horizon at evening, and later
the full moon shone in the mist
at my horse's shoulder so that he seemed to plunge
through a rocking surf of light. I lay in the arms
of a leaf-green man and floated in the trough
behind the waves.
        Are you ready?
                What happens then?
The long, gold light
of a low sun shining through glassy leaves
in another time – oh, hundreds
of years ago – where two mounted figures
gallop away down a shadowy alley of branches
in a *tapisserie verdure*.
        The branches caught
at my hands, the leaves
blinded me. When you are flying,
you should always hold on tight to the angel
whose wings are carrying you.
And still, you know, you could fall;
you might suddenly find yourself on the ground
with blood in your mouth, and your eyes snapped open wide.

Chapter Four: Early Sunlight

Married so few years, she begged him to stay home at night
at least sometimes – maybe three times a week?
She knew he had to go out often to Mexican bars
but to what, improve his Spanish?
                              Live a man's life?
She could never quite imagine it: the beers, the gritty wind at the street
     corners,
the old snapshot of copulating donkeys stuck to the mirror,
the barmaids – "My name is Living Room . . ." – stray dogs, a bloody
     handprint
on the wall a foot above the floor.
                              Their eldest child
was two then. At home, she played the piano
with that first child in her lap, the next
hanging onto the bench, the third poised
inside her, head down, ready to dive
into this world.
          "There is a garden
in her face," she sang as she picked white roses
in front of the castor bean plants at the ditch. She was living
contained in the ordinary domestic dream,
the early stage scenery of the senses. When she walked
down the stone stairs in the lawn, her long blue smock
puffed out a little at her heels
like Ophelia's skirts holding her up, or clouds
brushed under angels' feet, and she could have stayed
with one foot up forever, treading thin air.
                              But quite soon
the scene changes. It's a gray dawn. The new baby
is already born. She sits by the window
nursing him and listening to crows caw
as they fly up the cold barley fields

from the cottonwoods by the river. The baby makes
his tiny whimpers of pleasure. She looks over
at her husband lying asleep across the bed.
No fear of waking him up – he's just come in.
He is restless lately, and he seldom
gets home before dawn.
                              There must be more
to this story, I think, there must be a reason
for that girl to go on sitting there rubbing her eyes
as the light grows stronger, that young man
to turn over on the bed and fling
his arm across his face. Now the early sunlight
fills the tops of the pepper trees, the sparrows twitter
in the eaves of the house, the little children stand up
in their cribs in the next room, the horses walk
across the slope throwing long shadows.
                              A jackrabbit
jumps straight up out of the green barley standing
in the field. He looks around anxiously. His eye
is wide and bright.

He is looking at everything.

Chapter Five: The Night Wind

Darkness is coming at last, and the yellow evening star
hangs brightening in the west like a glow-worm in a jar.
The children's high voices shriek, their bare feet rush, they play
fiercely; they stretch the cool hour caught between night and day.
The horses stamp at their manger, the hens fly up to the trees.
Now there is wind in the garden and no more droning of bees,
and the night wind says, "Mount and go. See the notch of the pass?
You must cross and ride away through a thousand miles of blowing grass."

Chapter Six: The Ear of Night

While the sun sets, the whole world turns to gold
for a moment. The little bantam hens cackle
as they fly up to roost in the live-oak bushes, the horses
champ at their evening grain, the dog
follows the housewife back and forth as she moves
between the children's rooms.
                                        Far have I sought
for thee, long have I wrought for thee,
near am I brought to thee, she sings
to her four children, sitting on their beds
at nightfall, telling them an old,
old story, *Black bull o' Norrowa,*
wilt thou say naught to me? – and eventually
the soul's song is heard, it penetrates the chambers
of an ear, sometimes the hairy, black ear
of the bull, like the ear of night, sometimes
the whorled human ear of a prince
who is under spells.
                              And then he wakes up, just in time,
to the voice of the lover who has been following him
through glens, and over bens, and up the glass mountain,
wearing out seven pairs of iron shoes as she hurried
after him. He turns to her, and they tell each other
everything that has happened.
                                        As she speaks,
the woman's voice shakes. The children always hate it
when it does that, their backs wriggle
in protest, and they say, "Oh, *Mother,*"
reproachfully, but she steadies her tone
to finish with the black bull and the widow's daughter
living happily ever after; and then the children
are satisfied, they curl up in their beds
and fall asleep.

Meanwhile, their father,
in need of a rough edge as well as something to drink,
has gone off to the back room of a bar
named "The Midway," where he is descending
through many thick glass pitchers
of beer with a noisy group
of companions – including the department secretary,
a girl called The Black Rose – and singing,
very loudly, a Mexican song
that says the bed must be made of stone
and the pillow, also,
of stone, and that the woman
who wants him must really want him.
                                        The small stars
cross slowly above the roof. At two,
the people who are left turn off the lights
and linger in the darkness quietly finishing
their drinks. His hand slides under
The Black Rose's breast. Outside, on Highway 66,
the eighteen-wheelers roar past, heading out
through the night, traveling on, going
who knows how far, throwing their high beams
over the darkened ceiling and down the wall.

Chapter Seven: The Rat in the Wall

When she was thirty, X felt as though she had died.
For the place she came from there were many words
such as *blowing curtains, ash trees, weathervanes, stars*.
For the place she went into there are no words.
The people cannot speak, they shriek or mew.

Why, then, should she tell of such a place?
Why not be silent, being already voiceless?
She can't help trying to talk, although she knows
it seems to everyone that what they hear
is only the faint squeaking of a rat in the wall
saying the wind is cold in the cranny, telling them
to fill their beds with music and fire, to make
the most of whatever fates their lives allow.

Chapter Eight: The Glass Breast

Beating your white wings against the black ebb,
Be true to me still, my swan!
The dark water is a moving mirror
To tell me my young youth's done,
But yours you can see clear in my crystal breast
And what else now will show
The boy you were, the man you might have been
Ten years ago?
                              She jots this down
on the back of a grocery list, just a dramatic bit
of pastiche to relieve her spirits –
and certainly never meant to be read
by the swan in question –

                              who, meanwhile,
is driving off to teach with a brandy bottle
in a paper bag for his breakfast. His tenure
has been postponed for a year. (Too much swearing
in class.) He is not happy. He breaks
furniture now and then, he puts his fist
through the wall, it does not seem as though
he enjoys his home life much. He tells his wife
he thinks he'll get a job
operating heavy equipment. Fuck teaching. He almost never
gets home before three in the morning.
                              At which hour,
his wife is astonished to find herself
pretending to be asleep. Somehow, she never goes
to parties with him now; it's as though she couldn't face
the drive home at dawn any longer
with the old truck clear on the wrong side of the road,
and him at the wheel, his shouts reverberating
in the metal hollow of the cab.

"Practical politics,"
said Henry Adams, "consists in ignoring facts."
She is helplessly practical. She seldom
finishes her thoughts. She goes on planting
thyme and lavender in the sandy soil
at the edge of the rock garden, singing that she wishes
her breast were made of glass that in it
he might behold and see therein
his name writ large in letters made of gold.

Chapter Nine: The Past

The past is the severed head
of a rattlesnake.
                    It can still
give a mortal bite.

Chapter Ten: In the Corner

They are off in the corner
of the bedroom floor, red tiles
ten inches square, and he is banging
her head on them.
                    She has gone
limp, she has learned better
than to struggle —
                    but she lets
her sobs escape, trying instinctively
to rouse his pity.
                    He is drunk
but not crazy, he is punching her face
and arms now, but he won't
break her jaw.
                    As he hits her,
he yells in her face, over and over, be more
submissive, dammit, be more
submissive,
                    and she
can say nothing. She thinks,
but I am *utterly*
submissive.
                    It's not
true. She has never given up
a stubbornness, an unthinking assumption
that she exists, something she doesn't even
know she has — although he
seems to have noticed it.
                    But now
the scene is over for tonight, he's
passed out, she's crawling
into bed carefully.

                    The big moon
shines in their windows and on
the mountainside all around them, the same
calm light that has often beamed
on their bodies lying there luminously
conjoined.
            Now he lies on his back,
snoring, and she lies hunched over
on her side of the bed, her eyes wide open,
staring at nothing, her thoughts
veering in all directions –
like the last gusts of a storm,
full of torn off twigs and leaves.

Chapter Eleven: Inside the Engraving

Looking at the wood engraving, we see
the lane with its stone walls
falling down, the bare hill covered
with the fruit John Josselyn in 1689
called "skye coloured berries," the valley far, far
below with a lake in it like a bit
of white metal; on the other side, hills
black with cloud shadows, and then clouds
tracked through with more light.
                              In the middle distance,
someone drives a cart sideways across the high field
for ever and ever, amen.

Chapter Twelve: The Dining Car

The curtains close jerkily, this particular play is over.
The entertainment of the soul is through, the illusion
of a green heaven, all the painted landscapes, the clouds in tatters
trailing off down a river valley – we will have no more of it!
She will not imagine any more
that they might meet again, even just once (perhaps
in the dining car of a train
crossing the Rockies), and they,
two gray-haired people, might sit at a clean, white tablecloth
a last time across from one another.
                                 I think the train
pulls slowly up the long grade; it must have two engines.
Outside the moving window, there is a high, bare country,
its yellow grass bent over in the continual streaming
of the wind.
         At first, they're astonished
to run into one another like this.
He orders coffee, she tea. They begin speaking
of old friends, then they talk a little
about their grown children, avoiding everything painful
in their lives. "Let's not start blaming
anyone," she tells herself, "let's listen
charitably."
             She would still love
just to mention the warm stars like white match flares
over the Sonora desert, each one clearly
a universe in itself, and themselves, too,
lost to all scale, swimming
in the milky, uncoiling light, thinking only
of heaven, of nothing, believing it must all go on shining
forever.

But never mind that, never mind
the hunger she has carried for years
for some sort of blessing from him, a last word
that's a kind word. "Yes," she has so often
imagined him saying as he poured a big splash
of brandy into his coffee, "those were good days,
I never forgot them – " and she almost stops breathing, she drowns
in happiness, plenty enough
for the rest of her life.
                        Could that be true?
Of course not! Has he ever forgiven anyone
who turned him down? He is really
more bitter than ever. He'd like to make a last gesture,
all right, he'd like to belt her one –
                                and, meanwhile,
all around them, the stars continue their unbroken dancing
still, as if nothing had ever changed, could ever
change. Much farther than the farthest reaches
of any imagination, they trace their intricate patterns
in a balance that is always shifting,
and always perfect.

Kneeling Orion

Kneeling Orion

Two hours before dawn, and a lonely woman
wakes up dreaming the arms
that held her closely, still feeling
the warm shudder at the core. She dresses,
and steps through the side door, shivering,
to find her old car standing there,
glistening with frost. It's blind
with hard rime, but, as the motor runs,
she begins to see out by glimpses
into a black night where the half-full moon
set a long time ago.
                    The field track
rolls away under her past twelve ghosts
of titans, great bales of late silage hay,
lined up like megaliths clothed
in white plastic, mystic,
wonderful, shimmering in the darkness
as if white cows were lying there asleep,
looming in the faint light
of the stars.
            She drives on
slowly between field's edge
and stone wall until the stubble
ends at a rough slope where three does
leap sideways across the slant
in long bounds like the ups-and-downs
of rocking horses. By the headlights,
their eyes shine; then, in one indrawn breath,
they drop away.

What's below?
A slow stream flowing down the cleft
of the gully through its clusters
of wet woods, a stone bridge, a snuff
of damp earth, leaves
abandoning the tangled branches
of poplar and swamp maple.
                                    And above?
Only the brilliant night, Orion
kneeling over the black field,
his vast body extended, his bright shoulders
lifting his outstretched arms, his hanging sword
glittering before him, stars spilling all around
in grains of blue fire; and himself,
winter's giant, rising once again
into the autumn sky, brushing the bare treetops
with his shining thighs, filling the cold air
with seeds of light.

Sebastian

The riders go round and around the oval
of the indoor school like hands
turning about the elongated face
of a great clock, some hour hands,
some minutes and seconds. The horses' hoofs
are clear in their rhythms, the four steps
of a walk, the double beat
of trotting, or the anapestic triple
of a canter. I draw back my heel
and Sebastian strikes off; his legs say, *And the péak*
of the móuntain was ápples, his orange mane
ripples, his big red shoulders
rock steadily forward, his back lengthens
and shortens with each bound. As we circle
across the ring, I look up and see silhouettes
of bare trees in the narrow windows
along the sides. My eye
slides from the light
of the winter sky to the reflected light
in the mirror on the far end
of the wall. It looks like a painting by Degas
in there, horses and riders coming
and going, their shapes suddenly cut off
by the edges of glass.

Who is that
in a green jacket on a roan horse? For a minute
I escape the confining bundle
of identity – but then I see
that it's myself. There's a fractional
pause, a momentary
catch before it all
begins again, the hoofs surging forward,
the clock hands sweeping, my palm stroking the crest
of the old horse's neck, my mind saying, thankyou,
thankyou, Sebastian, I am so glad
to be riding you, to be hearing your hoofbeats
drum to me, over and over,
that *the péak of the móuntain was ápples*, that heaven
can only be now, something I hold
in my two hands, like the reins
stretched lightly away from my fingers
to your giving mouth.

Hearing You're Ill

Hearing you're ill, I remember
our defunct marriage. By now, we've been parted
longer than it lasted, but I dream at night,
you're in some kind of trouble and I'm sitting
by your hospital bed trying to hearten you, or else
instructing my dream lawyers to stop
bothering you. (I don't know *why*
they're bothering you; perhaps they're still combing out
justifications. Never mind them.) I had no idea
so many unsnapped threads were left
from me to you. And who is this "you"
I'm talking to, anyway, an aging professor
I've never seen, or is this "you" the self
of a younger ghost, some visionary reflection
from the back of the wide-open, myopic brown eyes
of a nineteen-year-old lit. major thirstily drinking
poetry in unfiltered draughts, riding alone
on the warm flanks of the mountains, thinking
about communal re-creation?
                                        When you reached out
toward her, her heart turned over,
and then sprang straight up with the leap
of a trout from pooling water, up
into the dusk of an April evening, so high
that circles from the splash it made, falling back,
pulsed out and out for years; and a few small ripples,
lapping invisibly, far in
under the chewed-out caves of the bank,
must still be whispering.

Riverside

It was all the love I could have. Babies
and houses, the house in Riverside
under the dry hills, orange trees behind it,
a running ditch in front, a barley field.
How can I not say "you"? I have to say you. It was all
you to my mind then, the you
I read Beckett to please (I didn't like him,
really), the you I gave
dinner parties for, believing professors' wives
could help that way (now I doubt it), the you
who went out to get drunk every night, the you who was full
of struggles I could never take in, never even
imagine, the you who hurried off
into the bushes with the Las Vegas dancer
who had married a physicist. Now I think
it must have been hard for you to find yourself
the anointed monarch of the imagination
of such a strong imaginer
as I was.
        I understand
so much more now. A lifetime
has gone by, you are far away, married
to your third wife, and I know you're dying, perhaps even
at this moment. Nothing is left
but the simplest reality. An old friend calls
and reminds me of how I took her driving
in the drop-front phaeton that long-ago spring,
around the backs of the Riverside hills, looking
at the blossoming trees, lemons and oranges,
almonds.

"A fierce drive,"
she says, and she tells me I never stopped singing;
that she thought I was going crazy;
that I had a black eye; that dogs ran out
to bite at the horse's heels and I beat them off
with the buggy whip.

Riding Out

for Susan Hertel

When the doctor tells you it's in your lungs,
you take the hormones he gives you, and also
the herbs and snake-meat the medicine man advised.
There are oxygen tanks by the bed now. After awhile
you feel stronger, you're breathing better; the dogs
get used to the hiss, they stop creeping around the room
with their tails down.
                        One of your children
comes from four states away to help you
and right away you get her to saddle the horses.
It's a warm day for January, almost fifty degrees,
as the two of you ride out. The black horse and the bay
are in tearing spirits, the dogs run, doves fly up,
hawks wheel overhead, the sunlight falls
sideways through moving clouds
onto red hills and blue mountains.
The horses dance sideways, too. There are deer tracks
threading the red mud of the arroyo.

"I was dizzy," you tell me later
in your happy voice, "the mane
blew back over my hands, I floated
on top of the horse, I felt as though the wind
breathed me, as though it carried me by itself."

Song

for Hope Nash

Two girls
coming home on horseback
across the wooded mountainside, too late
in the evening, and a doe,
red in her August coat,
runs across the track in front of them
from bank to bank of ferns
and off through the slanting light
of close-set alders.
                 "Don't worry,"
you said, "We can be as late
as we want to now, my mother
will be so pleased we saw a deer."

In that green world
under the clouds of branches
on the rounded sides of hills,
the deer are still grazing,

still pulling at the summer leaves.

Wanting to Have a Child

"Wanting to have a child," she said, "is like wanting
to make a garden." It was beginning
to be spring then, snow melting invisibly
from underneath, birds flying north at night
so high overhead that no one
could hear their cries – except, perhaps,
some man pulling on his boots at the back door
in the cold before dawn, going off to catch smelts
on the incoming tide.

Susan

"Yes," she said, "When the Gulf War started,
I felt as though someone had kicked a hole
in my immune system."
                              Then the long-cured cancer
jumped out from behind the door and went
for her lungs. There would be no more years
to paint, to see her horses and young apple trees,
her little, lonely house made of earth, her dogs
and cats, the serrated blue toplines
of the hills, the bleached cattle bones
in the dry river bed that suggested
enigmatic wings.
                              It was time
for her to leave the low, clear light
shining through her mare's white tail as it streamed
like cirrus, time to give up the shapes
and colors she loved, the way they all kept making
patterns together – the yellow wheelbarrow, the blue
door of the studio, a visiting daughter's
neon-colored shoes, creosote bushes, stars, snowfall,
fence gates, the belly of her black horse, India prints
lying rumpled on the bed, the full moon rising
huge at her window – even as they shifted
their positions, minute by minute
in an endless dance;
                              while her entranced
spirit moved poised among them, undivided,
filled with the same attentive affection she gave
to people, too – if they would only keep back
a little, leave her room to work, to be wordless,

to use her full strength trying to make each painting
contain it, give form to it, make visible
the moving, invisible breath, that living soul
she could feel within and without, that welled up
inside her . . . that carried her . . . that breathed her. . .

that breathes her still.

For So Long

For so long the tablecloth, the flowers
in crystal, nasturtiums and cosmos, for so long
the rosemary green on the windowsill, the migrating
flicker dropping into thick grass
with an underflash of gold. Did I think
it would last forever? I pretend
even to myself that I don't care
whether I live or die, but really
I'd rather live.
                    At sunset I watch
the half moon pause, slightly slanted,
over the stretched-out edge of hills
along this river valley, where the trees
have all turned into fountains
of stained glass – egg-yolk yellows, reds,
oranges – so bright that they seem like lamps
which go on burning for a certain time,
even while the gilded stippling leaches
out of the air, while shadow
tilts to dark.

Teaching Dreams

for Wes McNair

"I could never teach poetry,"
I thought, "and, besides, they only want me
so they'll have a woman's voice," –
but I did say yes;
                    and that night
a friend sat at the head of a long table
lined with pale, attentive students. He sang them
a carol about a meeting
with seven maiden saints *all under the leaves,
and the leaves of life.* As I listened,
I felt ravished with a sense of all-pervading
meaning
          and I stood up
in front of an audience, faces lifting
like poplar leaves in a summer wind; but my hands
were empty, I had no poems
to read them, nothing
to say. The silence
lengthened...
                    until a voice in the air
cried, "If I write down *everything*,
it will be poetry!" –
                    and I found myself
in a bed. Rain fell steadily
outside the French doors, a drowsy, autumnal
downpour. Two wolfhounds lay stretched out
on the rug. An unknown man looked in
and asked, "What is that music?
Have you got the symphony on?" Lying there,

I didn't answer. I couldn't tell him
that, underneath the blanket which had come
from my childhood, with its handwoven wool
dyed a soft green by the leaves
of beard grass, bird's tongue, and motherwort,
my knees were open and the music
that filled the room was rising by itself
from deep inside me, deep, deep
between them.

The Poetry Meeting

I went to the poetry meeting
bringing nothing but some Cherry Garcia
ice cream and a few peaches
from my little tree. I hadn't brought

a poem, I hadn't been able
to write one. The others all said
that didn't matter. I listened
as closely as I could

to their work, remembering
how the Buddha's ears grew long
reaching after the *sous-textes*
under the voices of everything

on earth, even the noises
of stones rolling sadly about
on their river beds. I drank
some white wine, I made

a few suggestions. Afterwards,
I drove home fast in big swoops
over the hills, looking up
at the moon – who was waxing

great with light, three-quarters full –
as she sailed past the broken shore
of clouds, filling the night sky

with her radiance, her assurance.

Lion

Lion, my best horse, it was long ago
that your legs were cut off
for the lines of student farriers at Cal Poly
to learn their craft on. But you were far away
by then, you had died in an instant,
a big slug in your brain, your muzzle in a pail
of grain, your jaws still champing. That was how
you ended, after all the years you and I
had wound through the hills together – on fire roads
cresting rounded slopes; on tracks snaking up
from the cool greenness of canyons, serpents
twisting among the countless breasts
of a red shale goddess; on deer trails
that terraced the brush beyond narrow streams
dropping over smooth lips
of sandstone and dissolving into spray
forty feet down in the warm air
of an April morning. Two red-tailed hawks
circled overhead, their calls bell-like
in the distance, and your four round hoofs
struck their eager rhythm from the ground
as strongly as your heart, which I could feel
beating steadily beside my left ankle,
swept us both forward.
                              Other horses
have always seemed like wind-up toys
compared to you. I think of you,
Lion, when I think about the luck
I've had in my life or when, in a storm,
the lamps go out and, in sudden darkness,
I hold a match to a candle until the flame
comes up with a yellow leap and the wax lies pooled
under the wick in a circle of melting light.

Morning

for Robert Bly

My cat, stuck outdoors,
jumped up and hung on a window ledge
with perfect success. His black face,
carrying a white, upside-down V
on its nose and fans of white whiskers
above its mouth, turned into a mask
staring through the window from the huge outsideness
of morning – snow, sunlight, icicles.

His success

was apparent in the well-schooled way
I rose from the paper-laden table,
and hurried, my slippers flapping,
to open the door for him. Time
trains us, animals train us, love
of all kinds trains us. Solon said, "I grow old,
ever learning many things." So do I,
although I'm never quite sure what it is
I've been learning. When I try to think
about the soul, I find my ribs expanding, my breathing
becoming deep and slow
with an undefined emotion, either fear
or longing. (Perhaps fear
and longing.) When I think about art, I ask
how I can keep some freshness in my work,
still, after so many years.

                    "You make it modern,"
said the flamenco dancer, "by revealing
yourself, not by embellishments. What's difficult
is revealing yourself." For "modern,"
read "new." For "revealing,"
read "loving," or perhaps just
"accepting." For "cat,"
read either "angel," or "devil." For "morning,"
read "the mysterious glitter
of another world."

Broad and Bright

September Twelfth, 2001

Driving to town, we passed two Holstein oxen
in their pasture, a perfectly matched
working pair. They were off duty,
quietly chewing their cuds, their black-and-white spots
almost identical, their four pale horns
tipped with the same black, their bodies lying close
in a natural symmetry. Long before,
they'd been paired up as calves and now, even when free,
they stayed together without thought, like stars
keeping their places by the timeless rule
of sidereal gravity. Their ancient, unvarying
ox-world of shouted commands – Gee! – Haw! –
of the yoke on their necks with the pull
from its rattling chain and clevis pin, the sweat
dripping off their muzzles, the nail at the end
of the goad, and then the ease
on the summer grass, followed by the peace
of the winter barn – all this
was double to them, two halves
of a nut in one shell.

      Seeing them there,
huge and solid, we pulled the car over
to admire such a Cuyp painting, still alive
in the twenty-first century. We knew the creatures
weren't troubling themselves with concepts
of time: no notion of being
anachronisms could ever arise
under those starry brows. They just understood –
in their own way – that they were two fellows
called "Broad" and "Bright," and that it felt good
to be lying side by side with a big pine
for shade.

When we drove away
I thought of how the Romans pictured time
as seven stars circling the pole star
in the shapes of seven black oxen threshing
the slow grains of the years. "This universe,"
says the book under my hand, "is somehow made up
of present time distended and stretched out
to eternity." I stop
to consider present time. What is happening
in our human world? Right now, during your visit,
we two old friends are sitting, one at each end,
of my kitchen table. The sun pours in
over the tablecloth, and a small bouquet of asters
nods in the middle. The radio clacks on
with its horrifying news. Meanwhile,
I read about the sky and you are refining
a clay head of Icarus, using dental tools
to show his eyes staring, his mouth wide open
as he falls and falls, full of the most
complicated and impassioned ideas,
through centuries of unresisting air.

The Last Week of May

I considered my death.
I knew it was riding toward me
like a man on a small white horse
riding through falling snow, but no faster
than the wild cherries were blooming then
by the ditch, or the old pear tree,
standing twisted at the bottom of the lawn,
went on opening her thick blossoms,
petal after white petal.

Hector

Shake hands with Hector the dog, for Hector is
not as he appears to be. He gives
a false impression by his yellow glare:
his glare is the glare of love, by love he lives.

Hector's well-bred eye is glassy with love;
he sees our presence and sees nothing more.
If left behind, he will go loudly mad,
crash through a window or break down the door,

and this has left him as scarred as some old courtier
who carries the seals of devotion on body and head.
He is always there. The king complains about it –
but he'll miss him once the old dog's dead.

In a Dream

In a dream, my terrifying father, long dead,
gave me a smile of complicit understanding, practically
a wink, when I told a tableful of people
he had written *David Copperfield*. Hardly!
And yet there was that smile, the amused, approving
way he acknowledged my mistaken efforts
on his behalf. Earlier that day,
I'd been telephoning an editor in New York, concerned
about a book my father really *did* write, worried
lest it go out of print after – can this be? –
seventy-five unbroken years
of publication. As it turned out,
there was no need to worry; it was only
a new edition coming on, and the last one dropping
into remainder.
                        The old wallpaper
in my parents' farm kitchen, the one with faded scenes
from Currier & Ives on it, lies buried
under many newer patterns. Would it even
be possible anymore to pry them up
and reveal the place where my father wrote
on the wall with his pencil (in Greek),
Be on the side of life?
                        When he died,
in his bed in that same house, all the lights
flicked off for a moment. His spirit
always *was* perturbed. I often think
how good it is that he doesn't have to bear
what's happening to our world (although
he predicted it). He would grieve
so fiercely, he would rage, he would tear
himself and everyone around him
to tatters.

       At least his words
go on being stamped onto pages. He would be glad
of that, and, who can tell, maybe
he knows it, maybe he's looking
down the field right now, just after sunrise,
from the farm graveyard at the edge of the woods.
Does he see his red house, the laden
apple trees, the long shadows, the deer
stealing in among the dry corn stalks,
while, below them, mist wreathes upward
in drifts from the black stillness of the lake?

Downstairs

for David Ferry

Scholars write poems about scholarship,
lightly disguised, as a way of climbing down
stairs, or the scales – or maybe just
the vertebrae – into the underworld, a hollow,
echoing place, lit by a few smoky torches,
where black poplar leaves drift downward
to the forgetful stream, and the gray king,
his head turned round to his back like an owl's,
stays close beside the young queen he stole
through the mouth of a flower.
                              Now they sit
together on their granite throne. I imagine
appearing before them. I bow low, I listen
to the batlike twittering of countless ghosts,
unseen in the darkness. I glance upward
toward the reassuring glow of Persephone's
thick wreath of gold wheat, then I reach up
to touch the narrower circlet
on my own head. In my other hand
I hold an engraved leaf of gold, my talisman
for finding the Well of Memory, for still being able
to cry out, *I am a child of earth*
and starry heaven: let me drink
from this water! and for making my way
beyond the fields of asphodel, that valley
of the soul – *the part which is not*
reduced to ashes.
                    In those twilit fields,
souls are winnowed by the wind, like grains
in the holy winnowing basket. Then comes the long
steep climb from planet to bright planet,

listening to their music, letting go,
at each shining gate, the deformities
of the life one has led. With the changing moon,
we leave our changefulness; with quicksilver Mercury,
our tricks of thought. Venus takes back
the ache of cruel desire, and the sun,
the unruly ego. We lose our anger
in the sphere of Mars; to Jupiter
we return our yeasty pride, and to Saturn
our hard judgments.
                The lakes and streams
of the night sky stretch out all around the traveler
like a dream, moonlight flickering in Virgil's
unsubstantial realm, where one wanders as if on a track
through a forest lit by *the grudging light
of an inconstant moon.*
                On this illusive path,
what happens? Only the divesting oneself –
slowly, slowly – of the stains and scars
of a lifetime. What remains? the life-seeds,
those sparks Anchises told his son
had the fiery vigor and a divine source – *so far
as they are not clogged by bodies*. Now the music
of the spheres fills the place where a beating heart
used to be, and its rapture overwhelms
the former mind. Does the hand still reach up
to the wreath of earthly gold as one plunges
into the way of milk, innumerable galaxies
flowing from the life-streaming breast
of an endlessly creating goddess? One is there,
at last, high on the road of stars
that wanders through starry meadows and where the soul

moves freely *like a crowned and dedicated*
sacrificial victim, at liberty
among gentle voices, solemn dances, and the majesty
of blest spirits and sacred visions.
                                        Plutarch
said that, but could he, or anyone else,
answer my question? I don't know.
At the moment, I am just here in the kitchen
on a dark November afternoon. Lamps shine;
fire whispers in the stove; narcissus bulbs
push their green shoots up in a stone bowl
set on the floor. Books lie open
on the table; nearby, the young cat
stretches out on her sheepskin cushion. Everything
in the warm room speaks of calm
and contentment –
                        and, meanwhile, outside the window,
cold rain falls on the empty fields, sinking
through roots, and rocks, and still-unfrozen earth,
into the currents of the rivers below, the River
of Sorrow, the River of Lamentation,
the Burning River, the River of Forgetting,
and the blue-black Styx, that dangerous water,
on which even the gods must swear truly.

About the author

KATE BARNES *lives on a farm in Maine that raises blueberries and hay. She has been writing poetry since child-hood and her work has appeared in such periodicals as* The American Scholar, The Kenyon Review, *and* The New Yorker. *She has four grandchildren. In 1999 she was appointed Maine's first poet laureate.*

About the illustrator

MARY AZARIAN *grew up in Virginia and lives in Vermont. Her woodcuts have appeared in Kate Barnes' pre-vious book of poetry,* Where the Deer Were, *as well as in* A Farmer's Alphabet *and* The Four Seasons, *all published by Godine.*

A Note on the Type

KNEELING ORION *has been set in Monotype Fournier, a digital version of a type cut in the 1920s under the direction of Stanley Morison, which was itself modeled on the types of the eighteenth-century French typefounder Pierre-Simon Fournier (called* le jeune.*) The current type, lean and sparkling, is as admirably suited to illustrated books as it was when it was first designed.*

DESIGN AND COMPOSITION BY
CARL W. SCARBROUGH